D0768832

Aircraft Carriers

By Virginia Loh-Hagan

Boulder City Library
701 Adams Boulevard
Boulder City, NV 89005
MAY 2017
DISCARD

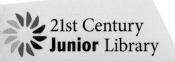

21st Century
Junior Library

Published in the United States of America by
Cherry Lake Publishing
Ann Arbor, Michigan
www.cherrylakepublishing.com

Content Adviser: Dr. Todd Kelley, Associate Professor of Engineering/Technology Teacher Education, Purdue Polytechnic Institute, West Lafayette, Indiana
Reading Adviser: Marla Conn MS, Ed., Literacy specialist, Read-Ability, Inc.

Photo Credits: © Derek Gordon/Shutterstock Images, cover; © Anton_Ivanov/Shutterstock Images, 4; © U.S. Navy photo by Mass Communication Specialist 3rd Class Margaret Keith/Released, 6; © Purestock/Thinkstock, 8; © Nevskii Dmitrii/Shutterstock Images, 10; © U.S. Navy photo by Mass Communication Specialist 3rd Class Lex T. Wenberg/Released, 12; © Stocktrek Images/Thinkstock, 14; © Rick Parsons/Shutterstock Images, 16; © U.S. Navy photo by Mass Communication Specialist 3rd Class Anderson W. Branch/Released, 18

Copyright © 2017 by Cherry Lake Publishing
All rights reserved. No part of this book may be reproduced or utilized in any
form or by any means without written permission from the publisher.

Library of Congress Cataloging-in-Publication Data
Names: Loh-Hagan, Virginia, author.
Title: Aircraft carriers / by Virginia Loh-Hagan.
Description: Ann Arbor : Cherry Lake Publishing, [2017] | Series: 21st century junior library:
    Extraordinary engineering | Includes bibliographical references and index.
Identifiers: LCCN 2016032393| ISBN 9781634721615 (hardcover) | ISBN 9781634722278 (pdf) |
    ISBN 9781634722933 (pbk.) | ISBN 9781634723596 (ebook)
Subjects: LCSH: Aircraft carriers—Juvenile literature.
Classification: LCC V874 .L64 2017 | DDC 623.825/5—dc23
LC record available at https://lccn.loc.gov/2016032393

Cherry Lake Publishing would like to acknowledge the work of The Partnership for 21st Century Learning.
Please visit *www.p21.org* for more information.

Printed in the United States of America
Corporate Graphics

CONTENTS

Aircraft carriers travel around the world.

What Are Aircraft Carriers?

Aircraft carriers are warships. They're moving military bases. They carry planes and jets. They're huge. But they have small **runways** compared to airports. To take off, aircraft need to gain speed. To land, they need to slow down. They need time and space to do this. Engineers study how carriers work. They design how aircraft can launch and land on carriers in the middle of the ocean.

Giant elevators, pictured here, take aircraft from hangars to flight decks.

Carriers have **flight decks** with short runways. At an airport, aircraft have about 2,300 feet (701 meters) to take off. Carrier flight decks have about 300 feet (91 m). Carriers also have a **hangar deck**. This is where aircraft are fixed and stored. On the side of the carrier is an island, or control tower, where officials control flights. The lower decks have special machines. These machines make carriers run. Lower decks also have living spaces. Many people live and work on a carrier.

An aircraft carrier is the size of four football fields.

How Do Aircraft Carriers Stay Afloat?

Hulls are the bottoms of ships. They're made of strong, thick steel. They float in water. They **displace** large amounts of water. Water weighs more than ships. Hulls keep ships afloat. They also protect against fire. They protect against war damage.

Engineers balance carriers. Islands are at one end. Flight decks are at the other. This design spreads the weight.

Carriers can go 15 to 20 years without refueling.

Carriers are big. They're at sea for a while. They need a lot of power. They use **nuclear power**. They have two **power plants**. Engineers carefully design the heavy plants, placing them in the middle of the carriers. They make steam. The steam has high pressure to rotate fans. Fans rotate **propellers**. Propellers move carriers forward.

Think!

Think about life on a warship. Do you think it would be hard or easy? You'd have to be ready to defend your country. You'd have to be ready to fight.

A technician must guide the aircraft into the catapult.

How Do Aircraft Take Off?

Aircraft need a boost. If not, they'll fall into the ocean. Engineers created **catapults**. Catapults store potential energy and release kinetic energy. Energy changes into motion. It's transferred to the aircraft.

Front wheels are hooked to catapults. Catapults thrust aircraft forward. Aircraft wings provide lift. Aircraft go 150 miles (241 kilometers) per hour in 2 seconds.

Engineers design a pulley system to move catapults.

Catapults are powered by steam. This happens below deck. Steam is pumped into a container at high pressure. It moves into several tubes connected to catapults. The steam is released. Aircraft are launched. Then, catapults are pulled back. The next aircraft is hooked up. Carriers can launch one aircraft every 25 seconds.

Look!

Go to your local airport. Look at runways. Notice how long runways are. Look at how planes take off. Look at how they land.

Pilots need a lot of skills and training.

How Do Aircraft Land?

Landing an aircraft is even harder. Pilots need to land at the right angle. Engineers design a light system. Lights help guide pilots. They let pilots know if they're coming in at the correct angle.

Crews lay out several cables. They do this at the end of flight decks. Aircraft have **tailhooks**. Tailhooks are at the end of aircraft.

Landing on an aircraft carrier is very difficult.

Tailhooks need to catch cables. Cables slow down and stop aircraft. Cables make sure aircraft don't run off the carrier. Cables are attached to special tubes. These tubes are below deck. A special system transfers the aircraft's energy to stop the aircraft. Pilots fly over the flight deck. Some pilots miss the cables. They fly off the carrier and try again.

Ask Questions!

Ask to speak to someone in the military. Ask if he or she has worked on an aircraft carrier. What was the best part about it? What was the most challenging part?

Try This!

Materials

8 popsicle sticks, 4–6 rubber bands, glue, plastic bottle cap, cotton or paper ball

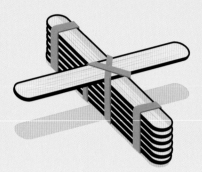

Procedures

1 Stack 6 sticks together. Put them on top of each other. Wrap rubber bands around both ends.

2 Place 1 stick across the middle of the stack to form a cross. This is the launching stick. Wrap rubber bands around the middle. Make a cross where sticks meet.

3 Glue bottle cap to end of launching stick. Allow to dry.

4 Create a base. Attach a stick to the end of the launching stick. (Use the end without the cap.) Use glue to join together. Place the stack between the two sticks.

5 Put catapult on a flat surface like a table or floor. Clear a small area. (Be safe. Don't aim at people.)

6 Place the ball in the cap. Push the cap down. Let go.

7 Observe what happens. Record distance. Record height.

Principle at Play

This activity shows how catapults work. Catapults store, transfer, and change energy. Bending the launching stick provides potential energy. Letting go releases kinetic energy. The energy changes to motion. It transfers to the ball. The ball shoots through the air. Can you get the ball to go higher? Can you get it to go faster? Change the angles.

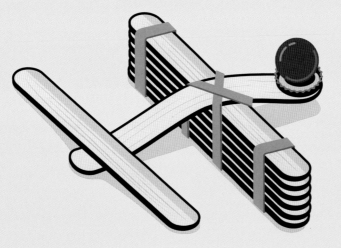

GLOSSARY

catapults (KAT-uh-puhlts) devices that launch objects

displace (dis-PLASE) to take over the space that was once occupied by water

flight decks (FLITE DEKS) flat areas that serve as runways for aircraft on carriers

hangar deck (HANG-ur DEK) place where aircraft are stored and fixed

hulls (HUHLZ) bottoms of ships

nuclear power (NOO-klee-ur POU-ur) energy or power produced by an atomic reaction

power plants (POU-ur PLANTS) places that make power

propellers (pruh-PEL-urz) devices with a shaft and blade that move objects

runways (RUHN-wayz) areas of land used by aircraft for taking off and landing

tailhooks (TAYL-huks) extended hooks attached to aircraft tails

FIND OUT MORE

BOOKS

Hamilton, John. *Aircraft Carriers*. Minneapolis: Abdo Publishing, 2012.

Nagelhout, Ryan. *Aircraft Carriers*. New York: Gareth Stevens Publishing, 2015.

Peppas, Lynn. *Aircraft Carriers: Runways at Sea*. New York: Crabtree Publishing, 2012.

Tagliaferro, Linda. *Who Lands Planes on a Ship? Working on an Aircraft Carrier*. Chicago: Raintree, 2011.

WEB SITES

HowStuffWorks—How Aircraft Carriers Work
http://science.howstuffworks.com/aircraft-carrier.htm
This Web site explains components and functions of aircraft carriers.

YouTube—Popular Mechanics for Kids: "Aircraft Carriers"
https://www.youtube.com/watch?v=RYWTYLsiFXc
This television episode takes viewers on board an aircraft carrier.

INDEX

ABOUT THE AUTHOR

Dr. Virginia Loh-Hagan is an author, university professor, former classroom teacher, and curriculum designer. When she taught third grade, she took her students on a field trip to an aircraft carrier. It was really cool! She lives in San Diego with her very tall husband and very naughty dogs. To learn more about her, visit www.virginialoh.com.